FROM RAGS TO JAZZ

Compiled and Edited by Stuart Isacoff

© Consolidated Music Publishers, New York, 1976
Music Sales Limited, London

© Consolidated Music Publishers
A Division of Music Sales Corporation, 1976
33 W. 60th Street, New York 10023

Music Sales Limited
78 Newman Street, W1 London

Music Sales (Pty) Limited
27 Clarendon Street, Artarmon, Sydney NSW, Australia

International Standard Book Number 0-8256-4066-0
Library of Congress Catalog Card Number 76-19122

Contents

Foreword

The thirty-three pieces contained in this edition were compiled from piano literature representing many of the major styles that have developed in American music since the turn of this century. These include ragtime, boogie-woogie, blues, be-bop, swing and the more contemporary jazz styles in which European classical harmony merges with that exciting rhythmic character which is uniquely American.

Many of the pieces are presented in a simplified form. Great care has been taken, however, to retain the authentic sound of each artist represented. The pieces are arranged in approximate order of difficulty, rather than chronologically. This will help the student to approach some of the technical problems presented by jazz styles in a systematic way (the technique required for some of the left-hand work in ragtime, for example, might be more easily approached after some experience with examples of swing-era music).

As an adjunct to more traditional piano studies, or as a guide to the jazz experience, this volume should be a valuable addition to the library of any intermediate pianist.

All I Had Is Gone

Perry Bradford

Moderate

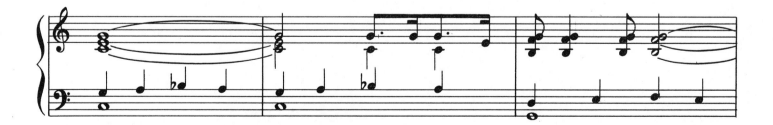

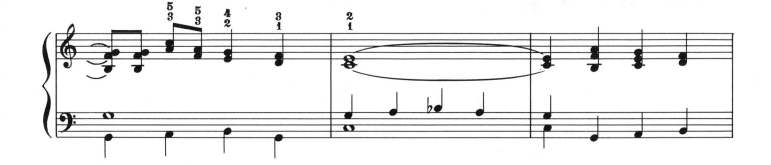

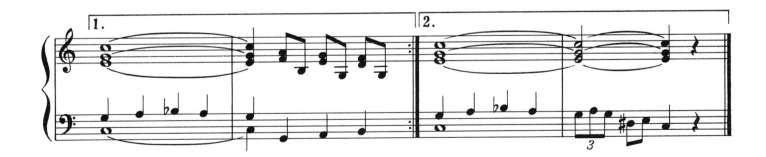

Ridin'

Willie "The Lion" Smith
Jack Edwards
Arranged by Stuart Isacoff

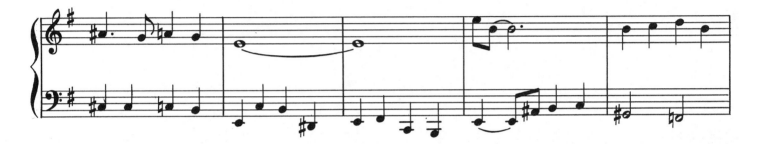

Get Out Of Here, Go On Home

Moderate dixieland tempo

Edward "Kid" Ory
Bud Scott

Justice
For L.G.

Stuart Isacoff

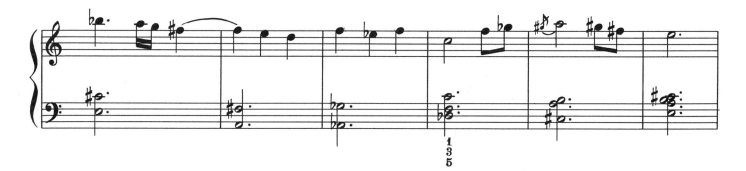

The Stanley Steamer

Earl "Fatha" Hines

Swingin' four

Ladybyrd

Tadd Dameron

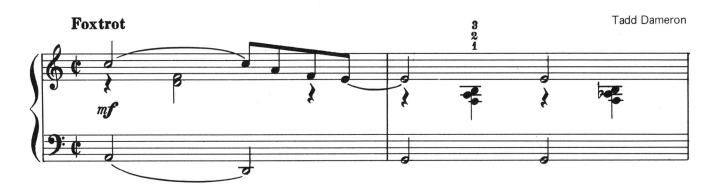

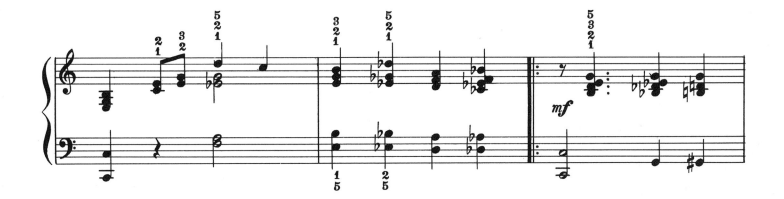

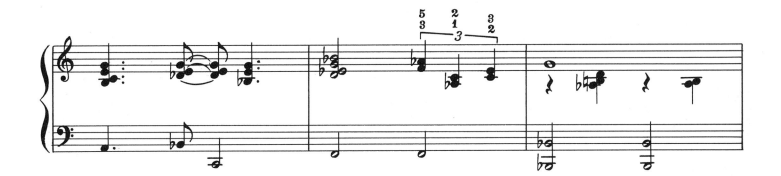

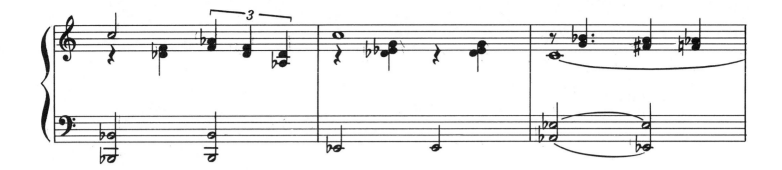

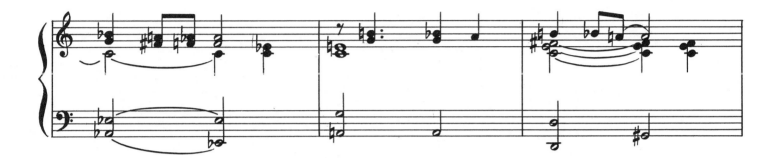

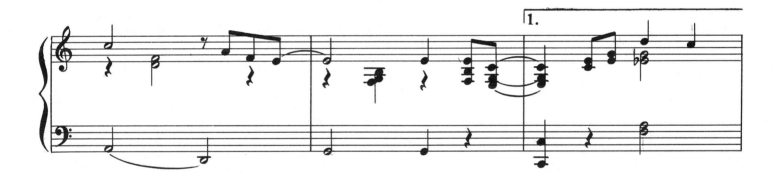

Blues Stomp

Traditional
Arranged by Stuart Isacoff

Medium

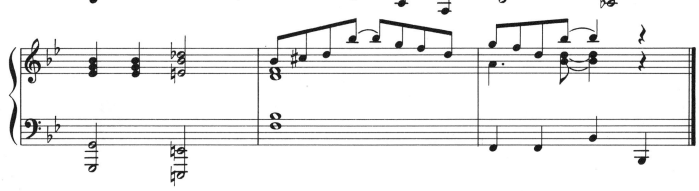

Ashy Africa

Medium

Percy Wenrich
Simplified arrangement by Stuart Isacoff

Spice-Cakewalk

Not fast

Jacques Press

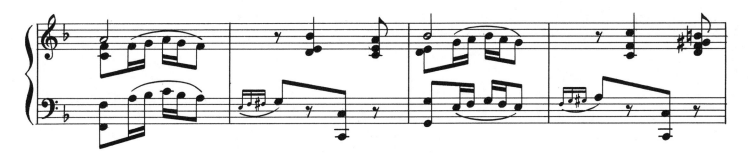

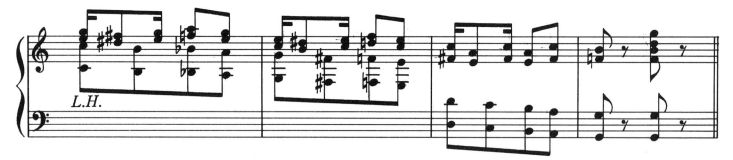

Coda

Swipesy

Scott Joplin
Arthur Marshall

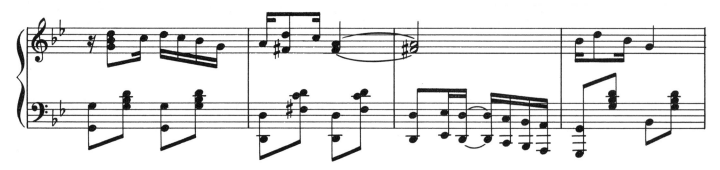

Back Bay Shuffle

Artie Shaw
Teddie McRae
Arranged by Stuart Isacoff

Moderate swing

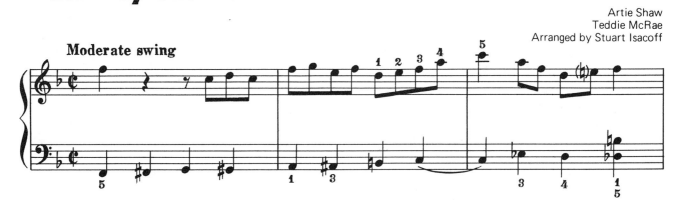

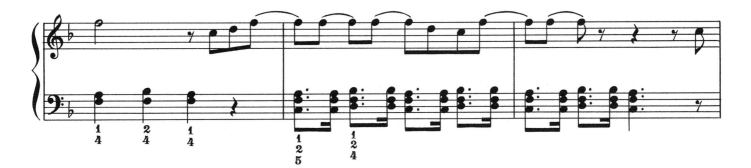

The Joint Is Jumpin'

Thomas "Fats" Waller
Andy Razaf
J.C. Johnson

The Toy Trumpet

Raymond Scott
Arranged by Stuart Isacoff

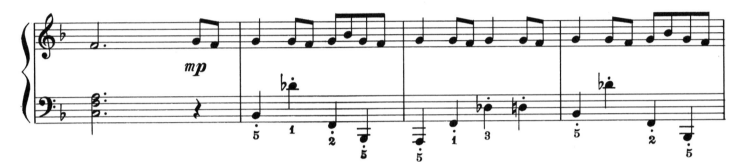

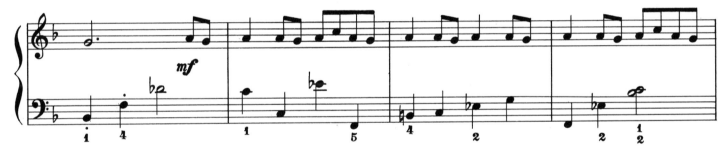

Mighty Fine

Moderate swing

Thomas "Fats" Waller
Andy Razaf

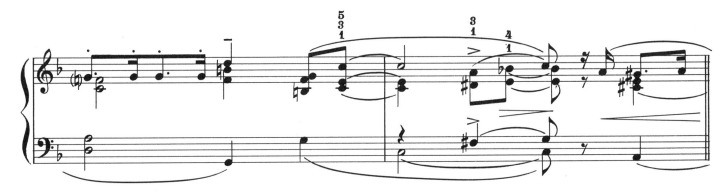

Nervous Blues

Perry Bradford

Blues tempo

Yamekraw (excerpt)

James P. Johnson

poco a poco allarg.

T.D.'s Boogie Woogie

Tommy Dorsey
Dean Kincaide
Arranged by Stuart Isacoff

Moderate swing

Pan-Am Rag

Moderato

Tom Turpin
Simplified arrangement by Stuart Isacoff

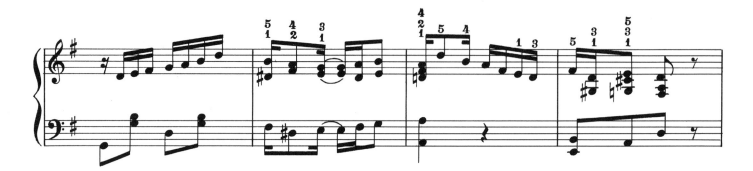

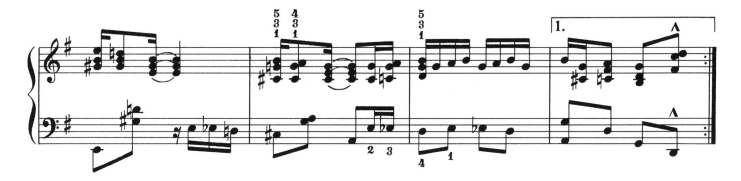

Trio

A Black Smoke

Chas. L. Johnson

Medium slow

Harlem Rag

Medium slow

Tom Turpin
Simplified arrangement by Stuart Isacoff

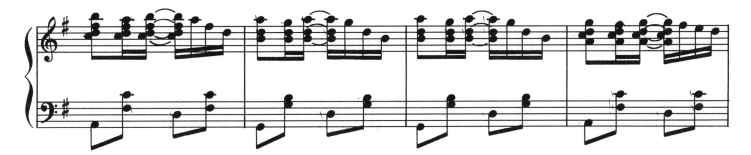

A Tennessee Tantalizer

Chas. Hunter

Moderate

Original Rags

Scott Joplin
Arranged by Chas. N. Daniels

Moderate

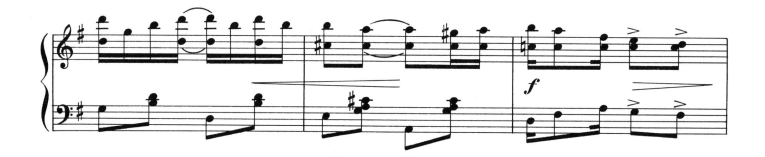

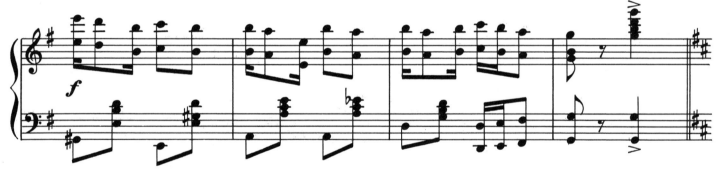

Off Minor

Thelonious Monk
Arranged by Stuart Isacoff

Medium fast

Between Sharps And Flats

(excerpt)

Willie "The Lion" Smith
Jack Edwards

Medium bounce

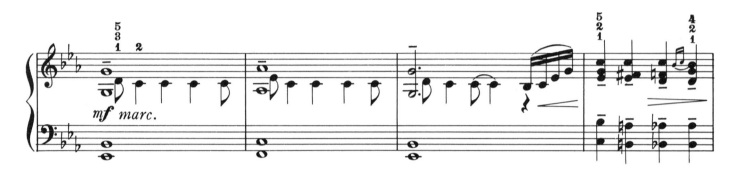

I'll Keep Loving You

Earl "Bud" Powell

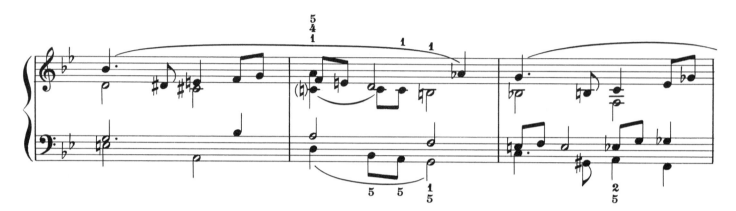

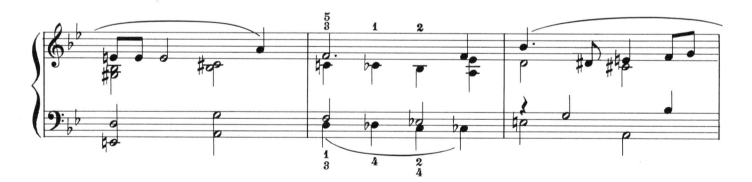

Monk's Mood

Moderately slow

Thelonious Monk

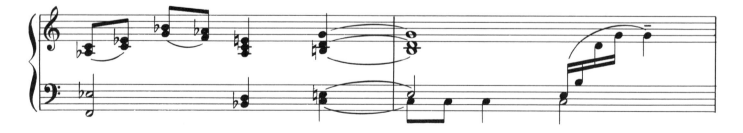

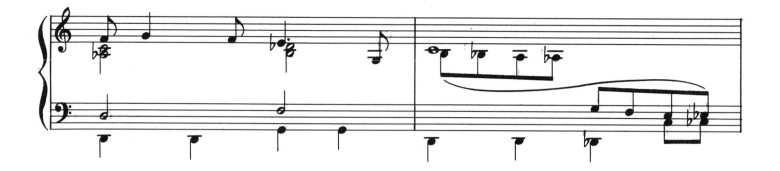

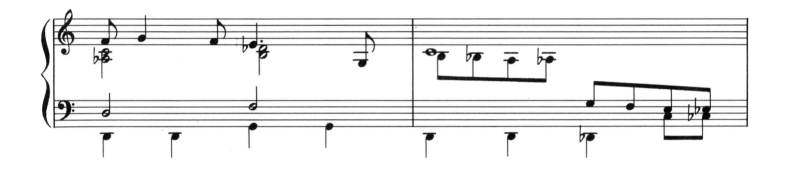

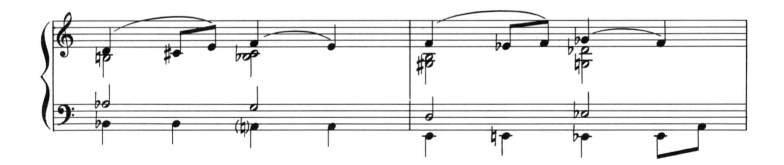

Monday's Wash

Erskine Butterfield

Slow boogie blues tempo

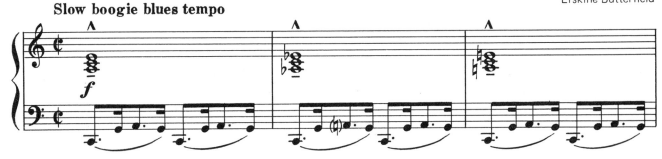

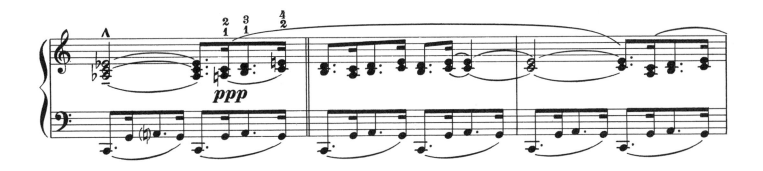

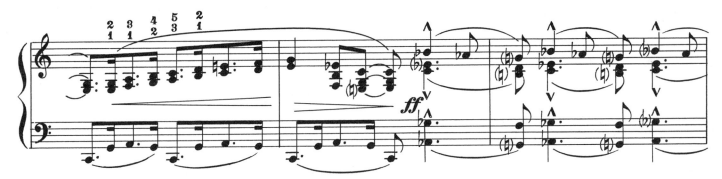

*If necessary the bottom note of each chord may be struck first.

74

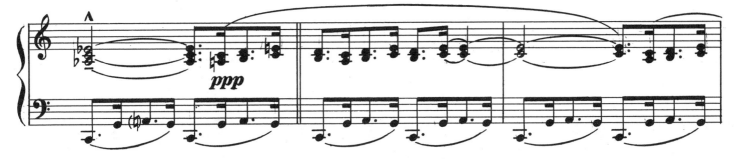

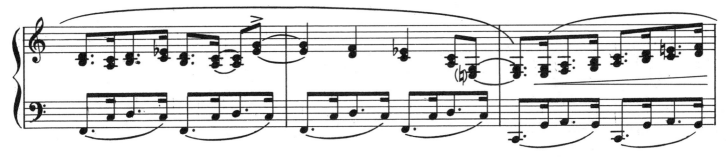

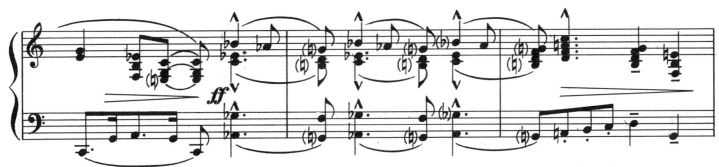

The Buffalo Rag

Tom Turpin

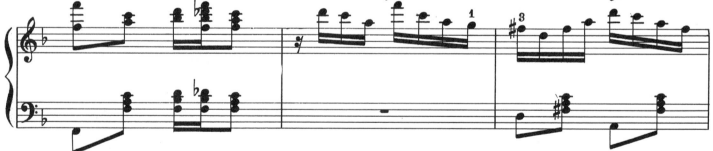

Piano Time

Fast

Erskine Butterfield

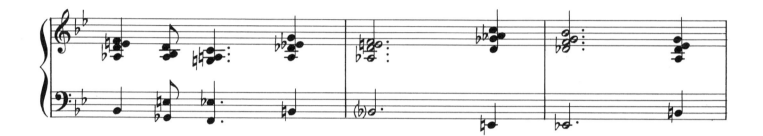

Wherever June Bugs Go

Archie Shepp
Arranged by Stuart Isacoff

Slowly

Sweet Butter

Erskine Butterfield

Moderato, quasi rubato

Allegretto e grazioso

Meno mosso e dolce

più mosso

Meno mosso

Più mosso

f subito pp

Tempo I

Snowdance

Stuart Isacoff

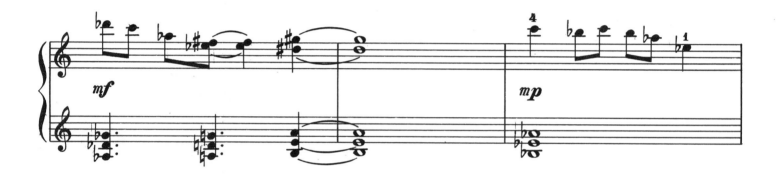

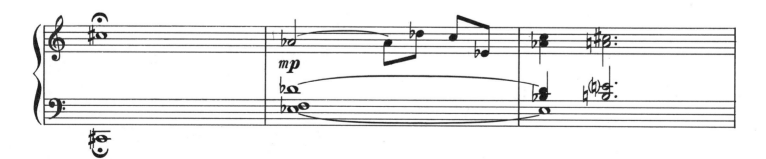

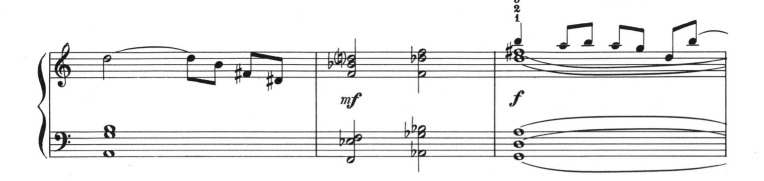

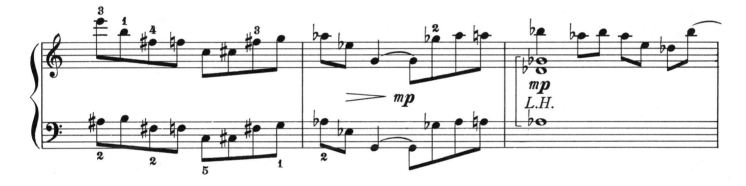

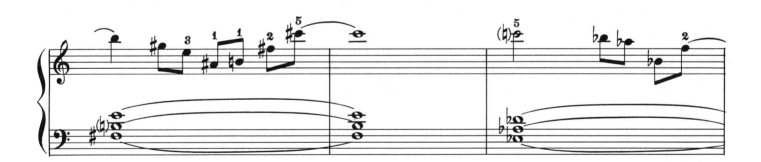

Lament Of The Lioness

Molto moderato e con grazia

Willie "The Lion" Smith

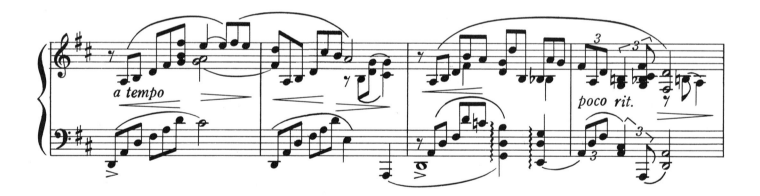

Trio
Un più mosso

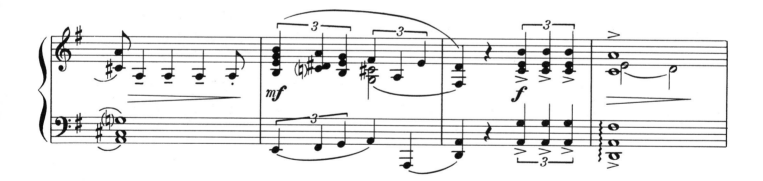

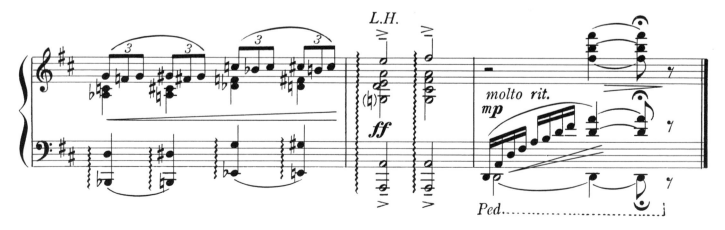

Index

MORE GREAT COLLECTIONS FOR THE JAZZ PIANIST